Places Of The Promise

By Susan K. Hedahl

C.S.S. Publishing Company
Lima, Ohio

PLACES OF THE PROMISE

9050 / ISBN 1-55673-231-7
PRINTED IN U.S.A.

For John and Katie
who inhabit the holy places
with joy and thanksgiving

Table of Contents

Introduction

The Incarnation of the Lord in the person of Jesus — child, rabbi, healer and the Crucified One — links our faith to human history. That history is particularly rich, for the holy people of God are inevitably the people of sacred locations. Places of the promise still enrich our thinking about the Lord who comes to where we are.

The Advent/Christmas Story is one that identifies specific places as the font of the rich interactions between God and humanity. They point and protect and reveal the events which are contained in God's covenant with all of humanity. The names of such locales are as familiar to us as our own homes. They form the habitats and geography of our spirits. Indeed, we see Bethlehem as surely as the town in which we now live. We know the uniqueness of its starry sky, the crowded inn, the sheep flowing over its hills.

Each of the following Advent and Christmas sermons focuses on the particular sphere God used to prepare creation for the gift of Jesus. The concreteness of location can serve homiletically as a trajectory for learning more about the sites of the Holy Land, the relationship of place to the meaning of events, and how God's consecrated places are linked to the blessing of the scenes of our own lives. Each realm yields its own unique set of symbols, memories and associations.

A. Sermonic Framework

The six adult sermons simultaneously follow three patterns. First, they move from the general, universal reality of God's gift of Jesus to the most intimate and specific places which comprise the Advent/Christmas journey. Secondly, the texts assigned to each Sunday are taken from the motifs of the current Year B of the Common Lectionary. An independent selection of verses is also offered. Finally, each place witnesses to certain clusters of names, events, personalities and directions which can provide themes-within-a-theme, for additional worship and homiletical expansion.

The children's sermons for Advent utilize the symbol of the Advent wreath. Historical precedence allows a variety of names for each of the four candles and their titles have been chosen in accordance with one of the ideas or symbols presented in the preceding adult sermon.

For Christmas and the Sunday following, either the Christmas tree or creche can be used as the primary homiletical symbol and focus.

Sermonic materials and biblical quotations have attempted to incorporate the inclusive approach to language which characterizes good preaching. Scriptural quotations have been taken from both the RSV of the Bible and, whenever possible, the *Inclusive Language Lectionary*. Sources have been indicated after each citation.

B. Congregational Activities

The following suggestions will enhance the themes of *Places Of The Promise*.

A worship committee for the season can be appointed in the autumn. Participants may wish to explore the following possibilities:

1. Designate a display center for the church narthex or adjoining fellowship area titled "Places Of The Promise."
2. Select artifacts, pictures, maps, audio-visual resources for the center.
3. Schedule parish events, tours and guest speakers related to the Holy Land.
4. Gather the following basic aids:
   - Map of the Holy Land during Jesus' day and today
   - Bulletin or felt board

8

- Slide projector
- VCR
- Tape recorder
- Bible
- Concordance

Detailed suggestions for use of these resources, as well as other possibilities, conclude the adult and children's sermons. At the initial meeting of the committee, participants can brainstorm additional suggestions.

• • •

As we enter Advent we know intuitively that we, like Moses, stand on holy ground. The following sermons name and explore those sacred places which form the crux and cradle of the Coming One. Let us go hither, to see what this place might be.

Advent I
A Cosmic Announcement

Series B Texts
Isaiah 63:16—64:8
1 Corinthians 1:3-9
Mark 13:32-37

Other Texts
Psalm 98
Jeremiah 33:14-16
John 3:16
1 Timothy 3:16

Good news cannot be kept secret. The pending birth of a child is such a momentous event that parents are often prone to telling even strangers, "A child is on the way!" Men and women begin calling themselves aunt or uncle or mother or father. Personal identities shift and change as the realization dawns: a baby is coming. If you have experienced this joy as a parent or relative, you also know the disruptions created by the presence of a new personality.

The forthcoming event is announced in many ways. Blankets and clothing of certain colors, blue or pink, are purchased. A special room is set aside in the house for the baby. Genealogical charts are often consulted, names are carefully mulled over and selections made. Before the birth itself a variety of signals tell the world — this child is ours and soon here.

God took elaborate measures to announce the coming of God's Child, Jesus. The Child's coming was not a maybe. Instead, it was God's promise, a covenant which would not be broken. In a verse that has been described as the heart of the Gospel, John proclaims the all-encompassing nature of that gift: "For God so loved the world that God gave God's only Child, that whoever believes in that Child should not perish but have eternal life." (John 3:16) *Inclusive Language Lectionary.*

11

But what was unsettling about the language of the repeated announcements was that this Child was destined to fulfill the needs and hopes of more than a particular group of people. For some that was a difficult fact to accept.

Yet, God has no special interest groups. It is a unique peculiarity of human beings to assume that their cause, their beliefs, their worthiness and hard work set them apart from others. From a human perspective, perhaps so. From God's perspective all of humanity is perceived in its equality — broken, alienated, in need of a healing word of communication and love. But where is such a word to be found and who will speak it with clarity and inclusiveness?

Forged in the worship and writings of many cultures, hints of a Savior were spoken in fragile, almost indecipherable form. When Paul visited the people of Athens, he reassured them of what their thirsty hearts already intuited — that the Jesus he preached was the One that had been among them all the time! "Yet, he is not far from each one of us, for 'In him we live and move and have our being,' as even some of your poets have said." (Acts 17:2) *RSV* Truly a word of cosmic scope! Certainly a birth for all seasons and for all hearts.

Alice Meynell speculated about the many ways God has been magnificently revealed in the universe and points to the particular cluster of humble signs which humanity has been given:

With this ambiguous earth
His dealings have been told us. These abide:
The signal to a maid, the human birth,
The lesson, and the young Man crucified.
(Christ in the Universe)

It is odd that the salvation of the world, the mending and healing of all the brokenness, can be accomplished in a baby. A mere child. The fragility and innocence of such a symbol and reality are almost laughable to us during our cynical moments.

Perhaps God could have used more impressive means to catch the eye and understanding of the world. Yet, Scriptures attest to the fact that kings and rulers and the strong armed forces of the world have consistently been frustrated by the singular personality of the Lord Jesus. One pagan Roman emperor muttered at his life's end, "Thou has conquered, O gray Galilean!"

The entire created order would sit up and take notice because of Jesus' birth. With both anticipation and awe the prophet Isaiah invokes the Coming One. "O that you would rend the heavens and come down, that the mountains might quake at your presence, as when fire kindles brushwood and the fire causes water to boil . . . ." (Isaiah 64:1, 2a) *RSV*

As followers of Jesus, we are instrumental in realizing God's dream in our world. When Martin Luther King, Jr. proclaimed "I have a dream!" he was ultimately acknowledging God's hopes for all of us.

And through our parish ministries (list here) we demonstrate that we have made commitments to God's people and dreams in the name of the One to come. Are there days when the vision is fragmentary? Yes. Are there moments when the work seems fruitless. Yes. Do the resources seem too meager? Often. But in Advent we dare to dream.

Humanity is sometimes baffled by the simplicity of God's actions. We attempt to make God look better. We wish there were something more than God's radical simplicity. Add enough ceremony, pomp, circumstance and adult response to Jesus and we might cover our embarrassment at regarding a God incarnate as a baby. And more often than not, we do succeed in wrapping Christmas with so many gifts, parties and activities that the season's reason is obscured. Yet, the cry in the night of the newborn child unforgettably reminds us of the orphaned state of our own hearts. We listen in spite of ourselves. His cry is ours. His destiny is linked to our future. The birth announcement has each of our names printed on it.

With utter disregard for boundaries, the Lord of the Universe proclaims to all people, through time and space, to all that is and is to come: My Child — for you! And there is no darkened corner, which will not hear the word of love spoken. No ear which will not recognize the familiar voice — and rejoice. A dream come true.

Do you hear what I hear?

• • •

Congregational Activities:

1. The display center can feature the different ways Advent is celebrated throughout the world: Advent calendars from Germany, Advent wreaths, samples of blue paraments, recordings of Advent hymns.

2. An Advent party can be held on the first weekend prior to the beginning of the season to make Advent wreaths, calendars and bake Christmas cookies. Children can help prepare the wreath which will be used during the upcoming Sundays of Advent in worship.

3. Older children can prepare luminaries for use in front of the church on Christmas Eve.

Advent I
Children's Sermon

The Lighting Of The First Candle: The Good News Candle

Directions: Wreath should be on a low table around which children can gather. Share the idea of telling good news first and then conclude with the lighting of the candle. Each question posed signifies an opportunity for children to respond.

We all want to hear what is happening around us. If we see someone whispering to someone else or opening a letter or making a telephone call, we wonder, what is happening?

Our parents, our brothers and sisters, our friends at school ask, "Did you hear what happened?" Some things are good to hear about and some are not. Maybe you went on a wonderful trip or maybe you got the flu and had to miss a party. There is so much going on in our world everyday that many people watch a program called The News in the evening.

Have you ever played a game at a party called Telephone? Someone whispers something in the ear of the person next to them and they pass it on, right around the circle of people. The last person says out loud what they thought was said. Usually everyone laughs because the news that started with the first person can become quite mixed up by the time it reaches the last person.

God once had some good news to tell the world. And God did all sorts of wonderful things to make sure that everyone heard the special message without any confusion. Do you know what God's good news was?

Yes, that God's Child named Jesus would be born and that this little baby would grow up to be the person who would make us all God's children.

15

Now there are lots of ways to tell people good news. We can tell them face to face or use a telephone or send a letter. But God told people that Jesus was coming in several different ways. First of all, God sent special people called prophets to tell the whole country of Israel that someone special was coming. Then God sent an angel to a young woman named Mary and told her, Mary, you will have a baby who will be important to everybody in the world. And finally, God sent a star, bigger than all the others in the sky. This star stayed over the place where Jesus was born. So the prophets, the angel and the star were all ways that God said, "Do I have some good news for you!"

A baby is a very special gift. You all are very special gifts to your parents and to us. And when a baby is born we say, "Isn't that wonderful?"

This morning the first candle we will light on the Advent wreath is the Good News Candle. And when you see it burning so brightly, remember that Jesus is God's Good News for us. It is God's way of saying, "I love you so much that I am sending the gift of this baby to you!"

• • •

Suggestions:

1. Mention some item of good news experienced by the congregation recently. The birth of any children in the congregation can be noted.

2. Any customs of congregational response to good news could be touched on; e.g. the placing of a rose on the altar for the birth of a child; the use of a telephone tree to relay information.

3. A new baby scrapbook could also be used in the sermon.

Advent II
God's Chosen Country

Series B Texts	Other Texts
Isaiah 40:1-11	Isaiah 61:1-3
2 Peter 3:8-15a	Ezekiel 34:11-16
Mark 1:1-8	1 Thessalonians 5:1-11
	John 1:29-34

You may have heard the words, "You have been promoted," or "You have been elected president." You may recall opening a letter for which you had waited and reading the words, "We would like to offer you the position . . . ."

Anyone chosen for a special honor learns quickly that it has both its delightful and burdensome aspects. Just ask someone who has taken on a new and more responsible position, and you will hear more than rejoicing about higher salaries or benefits. Sleepless nights and new decisions await the one promoted.

Out of the welter of Near Eastern tribes, the Hebrew people were chosen as the witnesses to Jesus' birth, ministry, death and resurrection. Israel was the land of salvation, elected before anyone even knew what that fully meant. The Israelites were comprehended by the all-powerful God as the recipients of an amazing gift. Awesome and burdensome. Hebrew scriptures repeatedly show that there were times of rejoicing and lamentation, even flight from God, because of their election as the Chosen People. With the loving eye of God fastened so irresistibly upon them, who can not sympathize with the joys and struggles of such a people who must have frequently asked themselves, "Why us?"

On this second Sunday in Advent we see a further unfolding of God's plan of salvation as the peoples of the world look toward one nation, the Hebrews, sent on a mission that would affect us all.

The sacred scriptures of the Hebrews are filled with an urgency and a gentler longing for something better. It became apparent through the centuries that the something would be Someone.

> *The Spirit of the Sovereign God is upon me, because God has anointed me to bring good tidings to the afflicted; God has sent me to bind up the broken-hearted to proclaim liberty to the captives, and the opening of the prison to those who are bound; to proclaim the year of God's favor, and the day of vengeance of our God; to comfort all who mourn . . .* (Isaiah 61:1-2) *ILL*

Special language and writings were used in the life of Israel to focus on the Expected One. The urgent speech of the prophets, the mystical songs of the poets of God, the everyday prayers of a yearning people formed the daily vocabulary of those waiting for a revelation. Messiah, Anointed One, Emmanuel, Son of man, were phrases which marked Hebrew life in worship and discussion. Surely no child had so many names chosen for him.

As with most babies, there were gifts to accompany the arrival of Jesus. But the notable thing about these gifts is that they were not only those of the Child, but earmarked for those who awaited him.

The gifts of God, originating with Holy One, carried the imperative of certain responses within them. The gifts of the Child would be the life-long responsibility and trust of those who anxiously awaited the Lord.

What were the gifts? The prophets of Israel repeatedly listed them, noting that the gifts were to be given away and not hoarded.

. . . the spirit of wisdom and understanding,
the spirit of counsel and might,
the spirit of knowledge and the fear of the Lord.

(Isaiah 11:2) *RSV*

The Coming One would bind up the wounded, welcome the ones who never thought they would hear a good word or receive even one good thing. He would do justice for those who had suffered injustice and insult. The godly gifts were given in abundance in the presence of the poor in spirit and the poor in material wealth.

In turn the Holy One would expect all of Israel to imitate this giving and abundantly pour on others what would be given to them first. The Gift Giver would be gentle and loving towards those in need and fiercely uncompromising towards those who refused to care for either God or the humanity around them.

Odd gifts. Ones that even the recipients might misuse.

Once in a local congregation a parishioner died who had struggled to attend worship but rarely could because of a lung condition. As a result, few people had the opportunity to know him as they heard his name prayed over Sunday after Sunday.

He continually recalled to the visiting pastor his joy at belonging to a Christian congregation. When the memorial sermon was shared, parishioners were stunned and disturbed to learn that the parishioner had been imprisoned during his life for a series of significant crimes. While they had rejoiced in his converted presence, members now had to think twice about the meaning of the promises of the Expected One who had spoken a word in the heart of one of their own. Would they have been able to speak the word of community and love, and share the gifts of God had they known his history and had he had opportunity to share it with them?

Can we extend such gifts to others? Indeed, we will never lack opportunities to give them away — to people in our community, those in our church. Perhaps there is a family member standing in need of receiving the gifts of the Christ Child, who asks us to bear them.

19

For our sense of expectation for the Lord must be fostered in the crucible of our relationships with one another. "Since all these things are thus to be dissolved, what sort of person ought you to be in lives of holiness and godliness, waiting for and hastening the coming of the day of God . . . ." (2 Peter 3:11) *RSV*

There has certainly been a clearer sense among Christians in the past several years about the nature of the gifts we might share with one another. Christmas cards, for example, will arrive saying, "A gift has been given in your name to the World Hunger Fund, or (name familiar church agency)." Christians are turning to those gifts, material and spiritual, which more clearly reflect the Lord they worship.

Peace-maker, healer, promoter of justice — our gifts to give in the Name of the Jesus Child! What a responsibility. What an honor.

So, over the slow pace of the centuries, Israel heard of the Messiah — in its desert areas, its little fishing villages, at the great temple and in the synagogues. Among the powerful rulers and the broken lepers and beggars in Jerusalem's streets. All heard, much as one feels the first spring wind and feels the joy of winter's conclusion. This child will be here — for you. And this child, like all children, will seek response to his presence, lives which daily and joyfully acknowledge the gifts he brings.

The birth announcements had gone out, sometimes in the fiery language of the prophets and at other times in the tender songs of God's poets. And Israel waited, pregnant with expectation for the Messiah and his gifts, living with the grace and responsibility of being the Chosen People.

• • •

Congregational Activities:

1. A map of the Holy Land can be posted in the activities center.

2. Some travel agencies have rental videos of their special tours and a video of the Holy Land can be used as a feature for a coffee hour or potluck supper.

3. If any members of the parish have traveled in the Holy Land, they can be invited to host a travelogue for the congregation. If several people have traveled there, they may wish to combine selected slides for the presentation.

4. If locale permits, the congregation might enjoy a trip to a synagogue for a tour or to attend a service. For those planning such a visit, an orientation meeting should be held to familiarize people with worship customs.

Advent II
Children's Sermon

The Lighting Of The Second Candle: The Star Candle

In the first book of the Bible, the Book of Genesis, it tells how God made the world and everything else. It also tells us that God created the heavens and the skies.

God has made the sky full of light both in the day and at night. What do you see in the sky at night that gives light? Yes, and we human beings have even looked at the stars and made designs out of them, calling them constellations. Some stars in a group are called The Big Dipper and another group of stars is called Orion, The Hunter. They all look like certain shapes of people or things. In Africa there is one particularly beautiful set of stars that people call the Southern Cross.

Stars come in all colors and sizes. Some are easy to see and some are hard to see because they are so far away. But they are suns, just like the sun we see in the day. And they help us think about all the worlds that God has made with suns like ours.

Can you think of places that the shape of stars is used? Yes, in school when someone gets a good grade, the teacher might put a gold or silver star on their paper. Stars are also used to decorate clothes and jewelry and we think them so beautiful that a lot of people even put a lovely star on the top of their Christmas tree. Maybe you will bake Christmas cookies that are formed in the shape of a star.

Now God used a special star in a special way once. Do you know what that is about? Right!

In the days when Jesus was about to be born, people depended on stars. They were like big maps in the sky. People would take long journeys and follow the direction of certain stars — just like we use road maps. When they sailed their boats on the sea or lakes, they also looked up at the stars and used them as a guide.

God used a special star to announce that the baby Jesus was born. The Bible tells us that at that time the star rested over the city of Bethlehem and pointed the way for the people seeking Jesus.

No one had ever seen a star so large or so lovely before, so of course there was a lot of talking about what it could be. Who saw the star? Probably all sorts of people. The Wise Men saw it. King Herod saw it and wondered if a new king was in town. In fact, he called several people to his palace to see if they knew what that star was all about. The shepherds in the field probably saw it once they had heard the angel talking to them. Maybe lots of people went outside their houses and said to each other, "What do you think that could be? Look how big and bright that star is and it seems to be right over Bethlehem. What could that mean?"

When you go outside at night and see a clear sky with lots of beautiful stars, remember that God chose one special star and put it in the skies so nobody would miss where Jesus was in the manger. It is called the Bethlehem Star and it was God's way of saying, "Look right here! My Son Jesus is born!"

• • •

Suggestions:

1. Show children a star map, noting how the Bible often speaks of God who created the heavens.

2. Give each child a star made out of some reflective material to hang on their Christmas tree. Or the stars can be arranged around the base of the Advent wreath.

3. Cookies in the shape of stars can be served after worship.

4. Children can construct a star or stars to later be placed on the Christmas tree.

Advent III
A River Of Destiny

Series B Texts	Other Texts
Isaiah 61:1-4, 8-11	Psalm 126
1 Thessalonians 5:16-24	Romans 10:14-17
John 1:6-8, 19-28	John 15:12-17

"Shall We Gather at the River?" This is a favorite song from our American Christian heritage, catching up in its phrases all the thoughts and associations which speak of invitation, anticipation of meeting the Beloved One of God there in water and the spirit.

Advent not only foretells the coming charm and joy of the infant Jesus, but it is paralleled by calls to consider our destiny in view of this Lord. We must think twice about what this child signifies for our daily living. For what is this child born? Words every relative and friend may ask of a newborn. Indeed, we do not have to look far to find a response to the question of how we are linked together with the Christ Child.

Traditionally, Advent is pierced with the cry of John the Baptizer, holding court at the river Jordan. We feel the gritty sand, look at the small shoreline fish darting between our toes, see in the reflection of the water the flash of bird's wings, and hear a voice saying to one who stands silently there, "This is My Beloved." Did we hear only the reeds whispering in the water? The small whirlpools touching the sands? Maybe all of this is simply our imagination affected by too much sunlight and moving water. No, we hear more . . . .

The Jordan was not new to Jesus or John. Both had played in its waters as children in upcountry Galilee. The same waters Jesus swam in as a child would later be used to baptize him and send him on his mission as God's Chosen One. This is John's witness: "I saw the Spirit descend as a dove from heaven, and it remained on him. I myself did not know him; but he who sent me to baptize with water said to me, 'He on whom you see the Spirit descend and remain, this is he who baptizes with the Holy Spirit.' " (John 1:32) *RSV*

These traditional Advent words, taken from the beginning of Jesus' ministry rather than the time surrounding his birth, give more specific information about the destiny of the star-crossed Child.

They are words addressed to the adult as well as the infant in each of us. The banks of the Jordan saw both the man, John, and the Spirit of God proclaim together, "This is the One." Advent is seasoned with the cries of John, parting the curtains of history, and then bowing off into the shadows, making way for Jesus.

In Israel God's universal promises unfold in the early years of Jesus as he starts his ministry at the banks of the Jordan River, the waters of his baptism sending him on his way.

What do those waters of the Jordan foretell? Some years ago a popular song caught the attention of everyone, called "Bridge Over Troubled Waters." Jesus came to Jordan's waters and like a bridge between God and humanity sanctified that place and went forth to sanctify all of creation. Where there was illness, healing; where there was alienation from God, Jesus created wholeness and even the demons cried out, "The Son of God!" We see in the waters of the Jordan, the reflection of the One who came as a Child to redeem and to calm the trouble waters of our lives. We see the child become adult, taking up life where the cradle leaves off and the road to the Cross begins.

John was the last of the line of the prophetic voices. God would speak in John and then the final word in Jesus would be spoken. John is a reminder that Advent has a somber side. That while we rejoice in the fulfilled prophetic words of John, we know that the cross stands near the cradle of the Bethlehem Child. Called from the waters of the river, we ponder what mission and commitment mean, what the new birth of the soul can mean. The cries from the cradle and from the Cross are one and the same for us.

John's call for commitment to God is not easy to hear. In a season when we look forward to receiving good things, it is difficult to relinquish that which blocks an effective Christian lifestyle. John's "sackcloth and ashes" attitude can seem more like the threat of ashes in our own Christmas stocking!

Over recent years we have heard people encouraging the celebration of an "alternative Christmas." There are articles and books and catalogues which focus on the ways we can more clearly receive the coming Lord. Our commitment for this Advent season needs to take into consideration these contemporary prophetic words as we are faced again with the zealous commercialism around us. Among all the gifts we give, which are the good gifts? What speaks of our commitments and to whom?

John's words to heed the coming Kingdom ring out. They are fierce, insistent, an invitation to turn and live life differently than we thought possible. But we are not left floundering before what may seem an impossible set of imperatives. As Jesus emerged from the Jordan, we see the person in whom we may place our complete trust.

It is time to gather at the river and then to be sent forth — triumphantly, confidently, knowing that our baptismal destiny is forged for all eternity.

• • •

Congregational Activities:

1. The waterways of Israel, such as Lake Galilee, the Jordan, the Dead Sea, can be highlighted in the display area.

2. Baptismal symbols may also be part of the center.

3. For worship the hymn, "Shall We Gather at the River?" can be used.

4. A bulletin insert can list publications relating to celebrating an alternative Christmas.

Advent III
Children's Sermon

The Lighting Of The Third Candle: The Name Candle

Everyone has a name. Even before you were born, your parents talked about what to call you. They probably thought of all kinds of different possibilities. They might have looked up names in a special dictionary or thought about names which were special favorites for them. And when you were born, your name was written on your birth certificate before you left the hospital. You might have even had a little bracelet on your wrist with your name on it.

Do you know why you were given your particular name? Yes, sometimes we are called after people in our family like our grandparents or aunts or uncles. Maybe you have been named after a famous person. Names are very important because they tell people something about us. Sometimes our friends might even give us an additional title called a nickname because it tells others about a special quality we have.

Do you know if your name has a special meaning? For example, Richard means strong ruler and Susan means lily. Some names are made in America and others come from other countries or even the Bible. The Bible has lots of stories about how people received their names. Sometimes it was because of how they looked and sometimes it was because of the things they would do later in their lives.

In the Bible we hear about how Jesus was named. Some of the books even have long lists of all the names of his relatives.

An angel came to Mary and told her what to name her first baby. The angel said, "You shall call his name Jesus, for he shall save his people from their sins." Another name which Jesus would be called by was Immanuel, which means God is with us.

So as Jesus was growing up he probably heard his mom calling him for supper, "Jesus! It's time to eat!" or maybe his dad said, "Jesus, would you like to go to the market place with me?"

In the church we have a special way of naming people. Do you know what that is? Yes! You are right. It is called Baptism. At Baptism, two things happen. We are not only given our names, but God makes us God's child too, and we join God's family for our entire lives.

Everyone here in church today is part of God's family. In fact we keep a big book in the church office which has the names of all the children and adults in this church who have been baptized. Your name is in the book of the church where you were (or will be) baptized.

Now as we light this candle today, the Name candle, think of your own name and think of the Name God gave God's child — Jesus. Of all the names in the whole world, that is the most wonderful name of all.

• • •

Suggestions:

1. The parish record could be shown to the children, locating a name or two in the book of those present.

2. Objects related to the baptismal rite could be used, such as a bowl of water, a candle, oil, a napkin, a baptismal certificate.

3. Name tags can be made up before hand for the children to wear.

4. Everyone in church can wear a name tag for this particular Sunday.

Advent IV
Small-town Revolution

Series B Texts	Other Texts
Samuel 7:8-16	Luke 1:46-55
Romans 6:25-27	John 1:45
Luke 1:26-38	Acts 10:34-43

What do you remember best about the town where you grew up? It might have been small or large or in-between. There you were nurtured by family and friends. In that place the best and worst of life's formative events happened for you. Is the town significant for any reason? Probably not any more than Nazareth was to the unobserving eye. And yet in the places of our human community the Lord impacts our lives in significant, daily ways. Thornton Wilder's play, *Our Town*, poignantly emphasizes just how special the places of our daily life are, regardless of size or location. Such was the case with the town of Nazareth.

Nazareth? Where is that? A man named Nathaniel who eventually became a disciple of Jesus' asked cynically, "Can anything good come out of Nazareth?" The town has a name which means in Hebrew watchtower.

Nazareth. What was seen from that particular watchtower? It was a small town and, as Nathaniel pointed out, nothing much probably happened there to make it notable. But in its dusty streets a young woman named Mary was visited by a messenger from God and told some astonishing news. You will have a child, sent of the Holy Spirit.

The walls and fields of Nazareth witnessed Mary's response to God's gracious news. Her song of joy at God's victory and the blessing of God's people rang out.

My soul magnifies the Lord,
and my spirit rejoices in God my Savior,
for he has regarded the low estate of his
*   handmaiden.*
For behold, henceforth all generations
*   will call me blessed;*
for he who is mighty has done great things
*   for me and holy is his name . . . .*
                                    (Luke 1:46-49) *RSV*

Mary's song is revolutionary. For she sang to a God who turned the world upside down and would do so in the life of her baby, Jesus. Proud parents forecast great things for their children, but who had heard of words like these?

In a small and unnoticed village, the greatest war cry of all times sounded, as the words of the prophet came true. What would the kings and rulers of the day think if they had heard such a liberating challenge from the lips of a young woman, pregnant, living in an obscure Galilean village?

Mary's song is ours. She sang of the liberation for which we long — in our lives, our family, our daily work. And just as her child's lullaby began in an obscure locale, so often does liberation begin that way for us. It takes only a word, a thought, a deed to affirm a change in our lives which claims the freedom of the Gospel.

Nazareth is a sharp reminder that liberation begins in the small, quiet places. "It only takes a spark to get the fire going," we sing. It takes as little for liberation to encompass all of humanity in the person of the Christ Child.

The authorities and ruling powers even today are eventually forced to take seriously the meaning of Mary's cradle song for her coming son. Whether in Central America, China, Ireland, Eastern Europe, or places in our own country and homes, the One Who Liberates makes rulers tremble and humanity rejoice. And why shouldn't they? Listen to the

32

remainder of Mary's song:

And his mercy is on those who fear him
from generation to generation.
He has shown strength with his arm,
he has scattered the proud in the imagination of
*   their hearts,*
he has put down the mighty from their thrones,
and exalted those of low degree;
he has filled the hungry with good things,
and the rich he has sent empty away.
He has helped his servant Israel,
in remembrance of his mercy,
as he spoke to our fathers,
to Abraham and to his posterity forever.
(Luke 1:50-55) RSV

The import of Mary's song can not be over-estimated. It is no accident that in places of political and religious oppression, composers have their work censored and people are often forbidden to sing certain songs. As Luther once pointed out, music is one form of the Gospel — with all its powers to liberate.

Who would have thought all of this was occurring in such a small town? Nazareth was in its own way as insignificant as Bethlehem. They were dusty, out-of-the-way places which the rich avoided and where the poor made their daily bread. Who cared what the peasants sang in those little villages anyway?

Yet, Nazareth is holy ground.

It is there where Mary sounded her lyrical praise of a triumphant God. It is there that Jesus saw sunsets, played with friends, learned to pray and to work. He saw Nazareth humanity in all its everyday joys and problems. He knew of birth and death and the disputes and reconciliations which comprise human existence, for he was one of them, a citizen of Nazareth.

What did Jesus take away with him from Nazareth as he began his ministry? He may have looked longingly at the places of his childhood, remembering the good times in particular. He may have taken away stories and memories he later refashioned for the listening crowds throughout Israel.

Perhaps he recalled the man outside of town plowing a field, who sold all that he had to buy that field. It was only later everyone found out about the buried treasure.

He may have thought of his mother sweeping their small Nazareth home all day because she had lost a precious coin her uncle had given her. He still remembered the celebration they had had at the supper table when it was finally found.

The road to Bethlehem eventually returned to Nazareth. In its cradle of human community, Jesus grew "increased in wisdom and years and in favor with God and humanity." (Luke 2:52) *RSV* And as he did, his Mother, Mary, continued to think of her Child's destiny and to repeat the song of praise to God.

We might even sing, "O Little Town of Nazareth," knowing how significant its people and places are to the life of our Lord and to our lives.

• • •

Congregational Activities:

1. **Pictures of contemporary Nazareth and its holy sites can be displayed.**
2. **The worship committee may wish to plan a Near Eastern banquet, serving the breads, vegetables, fruits that people of Jesus' day consumed.**
3. **Pita bread can be used for the communion meal.**

Advent IV
Children's Sermon

The Lighting Of The Fourth Candle: The Home Candle

We all have special feelings about the town where we live and especially our house. It might be marked in a special way by numbers or your family's name or a sign nearby.

Home can mean a lot of things. It can mean the house you live in and it can also mean the town you live in. "Chicago is my home," we say. Or, "My parents came from Minneapolis." (name locale)

You do all sorts of things in the place in which you live. You can visit your friends, go to school, go to the shopping mall, go to church.

For many people, home sometimes can change. Today people often move around a lot from place to place. Maybe some of your relatives live in a different place than you do or maybe you have moved here from another place.

When people we love leave this church to go to another town, we have a service and take the time to say, "We are glad you were here for a while and made this your church home. We want God to bless your new home!" That is called a service of farewell. When new people come and live in this town and join this church we have another service of welcome to let people know how happy we are that they are our friends and neighbors.

When Jesus was a baby he and his parents went to live in another country for a while. He was about three when they came back and they stayed in a little town in Israel. Do you know the name of the place where he grew up? Yes, Nazareth!

Jesus grew up in Nazareth and he did many of the things that you do. What are some everyday activities that you enjoy? Yes, Jesus probably also did some of those things. He

35

played with his brothers and sisters. He went to school. He helped his dad, who was a carpenter. He learned how to pray and to learn about God. He went hiking in the hills around town and fishing in the lake nearby.

The Bible even says he was a very special person and that as he grew up in Nazareth people really liked him and liked to be around him.

The little town where Jesus grew up is still there today. When people go to the country of Israel, they can go to this little town and visit the very place where Jesus was a child.

Today when we light the Home Candle, we think of the little town of Nazareth and we also say, "Thank You God, for the place where I live." And we ask Jesus to be with us everyday in our homes as our special guest.

• • •

Suggestions:

1. Bring a telephone directory and show the children all the possible places where people might reside.

2. Use a map of the area to note where children live, particularly if the area is urban and made up of several major suburbs.

3. Show the children the telephone directory for the parish, and find their names.

Christmas
The Birthplace Of Humanity

Series B Texts	Other Texts
Isaiah 9:2-7	Micah 5:1-4
Titus 2:11-14	Matthew 2:1-12
Luke 2:1-20	2 Thessalonians 2:13-12

In the Hebrew, Bethlehem means the house of bread. What a wonderful poetic description of a dwelling place. I remember frequently coming home from school and smelling the aroma of baking bread, creating for our entire family a house of bread. It awakens memories of good food, a warm kitchen, conversation, fulfillment. Everyone who entered the house gravitated towards the kitchen for a piece of bread with melting butter and to enjoy that delicacy in the company of others.

At Bethlehem, at this house of bread, humanity is irresistibly drawn to share in the good news of God. All things converge there and our souls find their birth and their nourishment. The entire universe holds its breath in wonder for it is here and nowhere else that we know our names, and find our homes.

G. K. Chesterton wrote of the soul's turning toward Bethlehem at Christmas.

A child in a foul stable,
where the beasts feed and foam;
Only where He was homeless
Are you and I at home.

(The House of Christmas)

37

Who could have known when and where the birth was to happen? The inn was full. All the inns were full. Caught up in the crowds coming to pay taxes, Mary and Joseph were one family among so many, one more pair of weary travelers. Mary's desire to be at home at that time can only be imagined!

Bethlehem. So far away and yet actually in our very neighborhood.

Those longing for the Savior had received prophetic hints that Bethlehem would be an important location.

But you, O Bethlehem Ephrathah, who are little to be among the clans of Judah, from you shall come forth for me one who is to be the ruler in Israel, whose origin is from of old, from ancient days. Therefore he shall give them up until the time when she who is in travail has brought forth; then the rest of his brethren shall return to the people of Israel.
(Micah 5:2, 3) *RSV*

Wise men needed to get to Bethlehem and used a star to do it. Shepherds looked for the manger and had angels tell them about it out there in the countryside. Herod attempted to find what was so close by and missed it completely, despite all the wise counsel he received.

The King of the Universe held court in a manger and the kings of the world knew little or nothing about it. Bethlehem — so close and yet so far.

Journeys make us ask ourselves about destinations. What do we do when we get there? What and who awaits us at the end of the road? Arriving at Bethlehem may initially cause us some consternation, for we eventually learn that we do not have to do anything. We are at home at last and there before the manger we come — just to adore. No more.

Once there we are graced with the ordinary, as comforting as the aroma of baked bread and the companionship of those gathered. A mother has given birth and there is a child. Not much else. But look closer in this little town.

For his birth signifies the birth of our own spirits. The words of the Psalmist echo, "Create in me a clean heart, O God, and renew a right spirit within me." (Psalm 51:10) *RSV* Penitential words and yet these are also words of hope and birthing. For we may find at the manger what we had not thought possible, the re-creation of our own spirits there by the Child and because of Him! How impossible and yet how true. In the face of despair, lack of hope and the daily pressures of life, we come again to be reborn. With all our hearts, we rejoice in becoming, in this Child, "a new creation."

Somewhere between the star high above and the manger far below we also see something else with the eyes of our heart. We see a cross suspended there in the stars. We see, almost against our will, the earth prepared to go to war over this child. This Prince of Peace is given reconciliation as his mandate and inheritance to offer to troubled hearts and besieged peoples. No wonder that we listen so expectantly when we hear of this Lord's coming.

We see in the shifting lights of the starry night the King, the child Jesus, blessed, full of life and the source of our lives from this Christmas Day and forever.

Bethlehem. House of Bread. Bethlehem, our home and place of the soul's birth.

• • •

Congregational Activities:

1. Creche scenes from different countries can be set up in the display center.

2. To highlight the house of bread theme, the congregation can be invited to bring samples of their favorite breads to a coffee hour, each plate bearing a brief description of the bread. Recipes can be made available. If communion is celebrated, a special Near Eastern bread can be used.

3. Pictures of present-day Bethlehem, as well as any artifacts from there, can be displayed.

Christmas Children's Sermon

The Christmas Tree / Creche Scene: God's Greatest Gift To Us

Directions: Children come forward to surround a Christmas tree, with a manger and other gifts beneath it. Or, they may surround a creche scene.

Have you opened your Christmas presents yet? Some families open theirs Christmas Eve and some today. At our house we open our gifts every Christmas Eve and it is so hard to wait. First we eat and then do the dishes. After that we sing songs and finally we open our gifts. What was your favorite gift?

God gives us the biggest and best gift of all at Christmas. What is that? Yes! It is the gift of a baby, the Baby Jesus. Mary and Joseph must have been very excited and happy when their baby was born. Probably all the relatives said, "What are you going to call him?" And then when they heard they probably said, "That Jesus is sure a cute kid!"

Do you know why God gave us such a wonderful gift? God wanted us to know in a special way that God loves us. Some days maybe you need to feel your parents love you and a kiss and a hug from them can certainly help! God gave us Jesus because God wants us to know we are never alone in our lives. Even when things get upsetting and hard for us, we can remember, "God gave me the baby Jesus to be in my life, to be my friend."

There are many ways that we can learn about Jesus and feel that he is in our daily lives. When we come to church, we sing songs about him. We talk to Jesus which is called praying. Other people tell us about Jesus. We hear about him when the Bible is read. When we look at objects like this cross, and that beautiful stained glass window, we can think of him. There are many ways to learn about the Christ Child.

Sometimes gifts come in funny packages. Do you see where Mary placed Jesus after he was born? That's right. There was no regular bed, so here we see where Jesus sleeps, in a little box where the cattle eat their food, in a manger. We sing a special Christmas song about the manger. Do you know the title of it? "Away in the Manger."

Away in the manger, no crib for his bed,
The little Lord Jesus laid down his sweet head;
The stars in the sky looked down where he lay,
The little Lord Jesus, asleep in the hay.

The people who came to see Jesus after he was born knew how special he was. When the shepherds and the Wise Men came, the Bible tells us that they fell down on their knees and worshiped him! They brought gifts to him and his parents, but most of all, they brought their happy hearts.

Do you remember any of the gifts that you got last Christmas? It is easy to forget the gifts we get each Christmas, isn't it? But there is one big gift that God reminds us of every Christmas and that is Jesus.

● ● ●

Suggestions:

1. A picture of the Christmas story focusing on Jesus can be given to each child from under the tree at the conclusion of the sermon.

2. Children can help prepare the creche scene to be used later in the worship setting.

3. Children can be dressed as Christmas characters and present a brief, silent tableau while an adult or older child reads the Christmas story.

Christmas I
To Our Heart's Content

Series B Texts	Other Texts
Isaiah 61:10—62:3	Isaiah 11:1-9
Galatians 4:4-7	Luke 2:22-38
Luke 2:22-40	1 John 3:1-3

In the days following Jesus' birth, he was taken to the temple in Jerusalem for a blessing. This was no doubt similar to most parents' nervous experience of taking the baby out in public for the first time. Mary and Joseph must have stood out as new parents and, as new parents do, they elicited sympathy and interest of strangers who would want to encourage them and put them at ease. Biblical accounts tell us that two elderly faithful followers of God saw Jesus and responded with overwhelming joy to his presence there. Anna and Simeon each had heard God's promises of the Redeemer to come and had waited, in fact, spent an entire lifetime anticipating God's gift.

Simeon greets this child, whom he has never seen before, with words of joy and recognition:

> *Lord, now let your servant depart in peace,*
> *according to your word;*
> *for my eyes have seen your salvation*
> *which you have prepared in the presence of*
> *all peoples, a light for revelation to the Gentiles,*
> *and for glory to your people Israel.*
> (Luke 2:29-32) *RSV*

It had happened at last and Simeon instinctively knew it. From the minor references in the prophets to the final birth that changed everything, Simeon recognized that he had been singled out to see with the eyes of faith the entire scope of God's plan for humanity.

But what had changed in Simeon and Anna's lives? The announcement was finally followed by the fulfillment. The perseverance of faith had paid off. God's covenant had not failed. And thus the eyes of faith of both Anna and Simeon perceived the greatest of all paradoxes: by the birth of the infant Jesus, their status as children of God had been decisively affirmed. What was far off had come close. All the holy places converged in this fulfillment.

The promises of God often seem far off and even impossible. We may find ourselves seeking signs of their fulfillment in ways that thwart, rather than allow the promises to bear fruit in our lives.

There are those times when a relationship, a career decision, a dream, require creative waiting. It is then that we are most susceptible to forcing the issue and a consequent loss of hope. It is then that we will often rush ahead, destroying or at least delaying what we have worked so hard for.

Everyone finally left the temple that day. Anna and Simeon went to their homes and contentment and peace. The family of Jesus journeyed back to Galilee to await the further adventures of God in their lives. Other people in other places also pondered what had happened a week earlier. The shepherds talked among themselves in the hill, pointing out the path of the star they had seen. Herod's palace continued to hum with upsetting rumors. The Wise Men journeyed afar.

Some folks probably thought what they had seen and heard was just their imagination working overtime.

All left bearing in their hearts the accomplished work of God. Some knew it with joy, others with uneasiness and fear. Simeon concluded his farewell blessing of the parents and child, a blessing which acknowledges the impact of the baby on humanity.

Behold, this child is set for the fall
and rising of many in Israel,
and for a sign that is spoken against
(and a sword will pierce through your own soul also),
that thoughts out of many hearts may be revealed.

(Luke 2:34, 35) *RSV*

We, too, for another year, are leaving the cradle of the child and venturing out. What will this year bring? If last year was difficult, will this one be better? Will our prosperity continue?

What resolutions have been forged in our hearts for the new year as we leave the child's cradle?

There are some here who will not see another Christmas. There are others yet to enjoy their first Christmas. And all of us bear in our hearts the desire for lives made meaningful by the Bethlehem Child.

We leave with the gifts, accompanied by this Child, for adventures whose conclusions we know nothing of. What places will we journey to and through? Where will we choose to stay and what will we avoid?

The holy places of which we have heard and sung, pondered and prayed about over the past several Sundays lead to only one final place — the individual heart.

God's promises sanctify and make holy all the places we inhabit, but especially our spirits. Paul has called the human heart a temple of the spirit. As we continue our faith journey into a new season we think of the invitation we sing in this hymn. And we remember the Lord who initiated it:

Ah, dearest Jesus, Holy Child,
Make thee a bed, soft undefiled,
Within my heart, that it may be
A quiet chamber kept for thee.

(From Heaven Above)

45

Of all the places of the Lord's promises through which we have traveled recently, it is the human heart which is the richest and most complicated. Earth's holy sites make their contribution, call out our memories and conspire to show us the events they host. But it is finally in our spirit that we receive the Christ Child and live with His presence.

We pray that the places of the promise will lead us, above all, to our heart's delight.

● ● ●

Congregational Activities:

1. Biblical verses containing references to the human heart can be displayed in the activities center.
2. Bulletin inserts can be used featuring a wish list for the congregation for the coming year of projects, needed gifts, etc. The list can be prepared of both material and spiritual dreams and intended projects.

Christmas I
Children's Sermon

Theme: The Promises Of God

Today is the last time until next year that we will gather under the Christmas tree (or around the creche scene) to think about many things.

The time before and after Christmas is a time when we think about promises. Do you know what a promise is?

That's right. It is something another person tells you that you will receive at a later time. They are so important that people use different words for promise. Sometimes they say vow or oath or contract or pledge.

We spend our entire lives making promises of all sorts of different kinds to ourselves and to each other. When you were baptized your parents and sponsors promised to help you know God better. Maybe before Christmas you promised to give someone a special gift. Did you do that? Maybe your dad or mom said they promised to go on a long trip with you this coming summer.

Do any of you have brothers and sisters in Boy Scouts or Girl Scouts? If you do, you know that they make some promises, to work hard, to help each other and do the best they can. People make promises all the time. They make promises to God and to each other which they hope and plan to carry out. Especially at the beginning of each New Year after Christmas people make promises. Do you know what those are called?

Yes. They are called New Year's resolutions. Sometimes people say I will try to lose weight. I will make my bed every morning. I plan to get better grades. Most of the time by the middle of the year or earlier, people have forgotten about their promises.

God made a promise to everyone in the world a long time ago. It was something that everyone looked forward to. The Bible contains all of these promises. At Christmas we celebrate the fact that God kept the promise. Do you know which one came true?

Yes! God promised to send Jesus to all of us. No one has gotten left out. God did not forget God's promises. And Jesus has promised to be with us all the time, every single day of our life. When you look at the Baby Jesus there (in creche scene or under tree), you are looking at God saying, "Yes, I did that for you. I have kept my promise because I love you."

There are days when we think other people have not kept their promises to us very well. And that might be true. People sometimes forget to do what they said they would and that can be disappointing, especially if you were counting on something. But God kept the promise to us.

Next time you hear someone say, "I promise . . ." Remember that God kept the promise to send the baby Jesus to love us and be near us always.

• • •

Suggestions:

1. **Bible verses containing God's promises can be attached to the Christmas tree, concluding the sermon with each child receiving one of them to take home.**
2. **Children can be asked to think of a good promise that someone kept in their life.**

9 781556 732317